Everything I know about
TEACHING

Michael Gove

Chapter 1

Why teachers should read this book

Chapter 2

My teaching experience

Chapter 3

My preschool pick & mix

Chapter 4

Kicking off with kindergarten

Chapter 5

The perfect primary school teacher

Chapter 6

Dealing with parents

Chapter 7

Winning the junior school jackpot

Chapter 8

Why teachers admire me

Chapter 9

Secondary school solutions

Chapter 10

Off to Oxbridge

Printed in Great Britain
by Amazon.co.uk, Ltd.,
Marston Gate.